The Selfless Bliss of the Body

poems by

Gayle Brandeis

Finishing Line Press
Georgetown, Kentucky

The Selfless Bliss of the Body

ACKNOWLEDGMENTS

"Pigeon Toed" and "Reversing" appeared in ICARUS
"Feeling East" appeared in EARTH'S DAUGHTERS and FRESH WATER (Pudding House
    Publications)
"The Gum Tree" appeared in TATTOO HIGHWAY
"My Aunt's Shoulders" appeared in MASSAGE MAGAZINE
"*Mano in Fica*" appeared in RUNES
"Choking" appeared in GARDEN BLESSINGS (Cleis Press)
"Flora" appeared in WE'MOON
"Jacaranda" appeared in POEMELEON
"Pear" received Honorable Mention in the Thomas Merton Poetry of the Sacred Competition
"Onions" appeared in PUDDING MAGAZINE
"jellyfish" appeared in THE NERVOUS BREAKDOWN
"Climbing at Joshua Tree" appeared in NO PLACE FOR A PURITAN (Heyday Books)
    and is installed at the Visitor Center at Joshua Tree National Park.
"Buttered Women" appeared in HISS Quarterly
"Coast Starlight" appeared in LIFE & LEGENDS
"Billow and Flume" appeared in ASH & BONE

Publisher: Leah Maines

Editor: Christen Kincaid

Cover Art: Michael Brandeis

Author Photo: Rachael Warecki, CameraRAW Photography

Cover Design: Elizabeth Maines

Printed in the USA on acid-free paper.
Order online: www.finishinglinepress.com
                also available on amazon.com

Author inquiries and mail orders:
Finishing Line Press
P. O. Box 1626
Georgetown, Kentucky 40324
U. S. A.

Table of Contents

SMALL HUNGERS

GHOST

THE SELFLESS BLISS OF THE BODY

FLORA

SWARM

WAITING

WORLDLING

SMALL HUNGERS

Pigeon-Toed

I was born with my feet
turned in. Pigeon-toed,
the doctor called it,
as if I could bypass
creeping, crawling, walking,
and learn to fly, instead.
He wrapped my ankles
and feet in plaster
and gauze—
little stone booties,
little foot bindings
to bring my bones
back in order,
keep me firmly
on the ground.

Now my feet ache
to turn in again, return
to their original state,
my whole body arcing
to face itself,
twisting towards
its skeleton
in search of
the soaring bones.

The Chills

Concentrate, concentrate,
concentrate on what I'm saying,
babies are dying, mothers are crying,
concentrate, concentrate

My sister and I took turns
pounding the poem
onto each other's bare backs,
mindful not to touch the other's spine.

There's a knife in your back
and the blood rushes down
rushes down, rushes down,

We thought if we touched someone's spine,
that person would die, or,
at the very least,
be instantly paralyzed.

Bullets in your back
and the blood rushes down
rushes down, rushes down

Each knob of vertebra
bulged under the skin, menacing
as the bud of a new tooth.
We didn't want to hurt each other.
Our hands were careful weapons.

Crabs crawling up your back
Crabs crawling down your back
Crabs crawling up your back
Crabs crawling down your back

We thought we would die

if we touched the tender skin
of our temples. We thought our bodies
were full of danger zones, nerve endings
that would not survive
even the slightest nudge.
We stuck out our tongues
and touched them, tip to tip.
The resulting shock almost
knocked us down.
We knew we were electric,
lethal as The Chair.
We knew we had the capacity
to blow our own circuits.

Cool breeze. Tight squeeze.
Now you've got the chills.

Small Hungers

Once I asked my mother
if anyone in the world
had all the same
clothes and toys
as me—the exact number,
exact colors, not a single
ceramic rabbit more
or less. She said *yes,*
someone must, the world
is so big...
and as room, chair, name
stitched on my dress slipped
into vast impersonal horror,
she made soup,
she made a sandwich,
to feed my small hungers.

The Gum Tree

This tree did not produce
chicle or gum arabic—
it was an oak, probably,
or a maple, some normal tree
on Main Street
just outside the White
Hen Pantry
where we bought Fun-
yuns and Now
and Laters after school.
People put gum
on the gum tree—
the whole trunk
was studded with it,
wads of purple,
green, yellow, pink,
little wrinkles of Trident,
larger blobs of Bubble
Yum, some tongued smooth,
others still imprinted
with ridges of teeth.
I thought the tree
was beautiful,
a living mosaic, slightly
scented with mint and fake
watermelon sugar.
Each piece of gum
seemed like a kiss
to me, an open mouth,
almost unbearably intimate,
rubbery bits once warmed
by breath, slippery
with spit, the insides
of people's bodies
exposed there, the bark

pressed firm and patient
against them
like a tongue.

Feeling East

I used to think East
was wherever I pointed my right
hand. I was six, my body
the center of space, the axis
on which directions turned.
When I learned directions
are fixed, that our bodies
move through space
like fish, East became
the sunrise, but, even more so,
the lake. Around Chicago, Lake
Michigan is what is East,
and my body could always feel
its presence. Riding home
from the city, dozing
in the back seat, I always knew
where we were.

Living out West now, I find
directions hazy as smog. My right
hand points to mountains, to palms,
but their presence looms light
in my body. When I get lost,
and I do, I close my eyes
and try to feel East,
tracing sharp shores of memory,
the pull of the lake in my blood,
following the three right turns home.

Chute

It was a thrill and horror
to be in charge of trash.
I held my breath
whenever I carried
sodden, laden paper bags
from Jewel to the chute
in the sour closet
down the hall
from our apartment,
opened the heavy
chrome door gleaming
against the far
cinderblock wall,
and let the bags slide
to their doom.
The furnace rumbled
five stories down
as it ate old Kotex
and Manwich cans,
hair combed from brushes—
my family's hair, my hair,
burnt into nothing.

***

A friend at school
told me we hurtle
down a tunnel
when we die,
the spirits of our dead
waiting for us
with open arms.
The thought made me
dizzy. I didn't want to be
stuck with dead

relatives I barely knew,
didn't want to live
without my body.
I prayed the tunnel
at the end of life
would be more
like the garbage chute,
a tumble to a final
conflagration
into nothing,
into everything,
one last dark
and brilliant blaze.

GHOST

cubeb

(14c): the dried unripe berry of a tropical
shrub (Piper cubeba) of the pepper family
that is crushed and smoked in cigarettes
for catarrh

My parents took a Caribbean cruise
when I was in utero. On an island
stop, a bird trainer asked my mother
to join him on stage. Her pregnancy
barely showed beneath her pink
shift as she pushed through
the crowd. Flamingos
soon surrounded her, a flurry
of feathers the same shade
as her dress. She disappeared
into the birds, my parents
told me. Everything
but her head vanished.

Laughing, my mother stepped
back into the audience, back
into her own silhouette.
She pulled a cigarette
from her purse. My dad
lit it for her, kissed her flushed face
as the flamingos were ushered away,
as the unripe berry of my body
took in threads of smoke, clouds
a magician uses to make someone
disappear.

Amoeba

Driving with a clutch
of high school friends,
one asked: *What prehistoric
creature would you be?*
T-Rex, friends shouted,
Triceratops, Pterandon, all
large creatures with tough skin,
sharp teeth, abundant muscle.
The thought of living
in such vicious bodies
made me cringe. *I would
be an amoeba*, I said,
making my friends laugh,
call me a weirdo
as we sped down the street.
*Why do you always want
to disappear?* they asked—
a question I still sometimes ask
myself—but a whole lifetime later,
I would choose amoeba again, body
condensed to a singular gleaming,
a pulse of pure movement, workings
shining though translucent skin.

Reversing

The first time I parked with a boy,
I stayed in the driver's seat,
my seat belt still buckled,
my other one not.
It wasn't *parking*, technically—
for some reason, I kept the gear
in reverse the entire time,
kept my foot on the brake
while we steamed up
the windows
and a thick lake fog
clouded the body of the car—
as if in all that vapor
I needed to keep my foot
on something solid,
something that could send me
down a defined path
so I wouldn't float away,
a Chagall woman
bent like a comma
in the air, drifting off
on tendrils of sky.

yours in the void

as a child, i loved
learning about factories—
potato chips, shoes,
coming into being,
their beautiful, impersonal,
forming—but i wanted
to go back even further...
what farm, what seed, what cow,
what tree, what rain, what salt,
what hands...to trace the process
to its initial empty source.

　　　*

i have heard:

　　　　in the center

　　　　　　of the earth

　　　　　　　　there is fire

　　　　　in the center

　　　　of the fire

silence

　　　*

do you know
as you touch

my neck, you are touching
emptiness, that i am
invisible in the middle,
that i am only yours
in the void?

Ghost

My hand is light
with the pen; words often
don't reach the carbons below
the paper—the yellow layer
of permission slips, the copies
of all my checks, look
like they've been breathed on
by just a pale sister of ink.
I have to squint to remember
what I've bought, what I've bought into.

My voice is soft; answering
machines often don't pick it up—
they hang up on me just as I'm about
to say my name. My friends know
it's me when the message
clicks off after "Hi" or "This".
At readings, people often ask me
to speak up. I say "I'll try", and I do,
but even then, some members
of the audience still have to
bend forward to hear.

I used to freak out my sister
by telling her I wasn't
Gayle, I was the ghost of Gayle.
Sometimes I worry I have become
that ghost, just a pale sister
of my possible self, a whisper
of who I could be, but I know I am
most at home on the verge
of dissolution, the tingle
of almost-not-being
everpresent in my bones.

Detail

I leave big holes
when I write.
I leave notes
(more here)
to remind myself
to fill in the gaps,
plug in the characters'
hair color, the temperature
of the room, the *(more
here)*. Sometimes I forget
to go back and add detail;
sometimes I am scared
to get so close.

(more here)

My friend took a sculpture
class; his clay heads
and torsos were smeary
and abstract. *You don't
go for the detail, do you?*
his instructor assessed—
*you go straight for the essence
of the person.* My friend
wasn't sure. He thought
maybe his hands just weren't
skilled enough to find the true
shape of the face—
the precise bump
on the bridge of the nose,
the crease on each side
of the lips, the *(more here)*.
It was easier to scrunch out
a shaggy aura, blurry edges.

(more here)

If God is
in the details…

(more here)

A writer told me she keeps
a cardboard toilet paper tube
by her keyboard.
Every once in a while
she picks it up
and looks through it
like a monocular.
It reminds her to look
closer at what she is writing,
to zoom down
to the smallest detail.
I am more comfortable
in the big picture; I like
sliding around that spacious
field. Putting a tube
to my eye almost hurts.

(more here)

If the Devil is
in the details…

(more here)

Sometimes I forget
who I am. I feel
alien inside my skin.
I can't quite believe

this is my life. I feel
on the brink of nothingness,
like I'm going
to dissolve into some bouillon
of collective unconscious
and not be able to find
my way back to this
body, this family.
It is the details—
the birthmark
near my temple,
the curved scar
on my knee
the taste of my tongue
(more)
that finally save me,
it is the details—
why am I afraid
to admit this?—
it is the details
that bring me back
where I belong
(here)

THE SELFLESS BLISS OF THE BODY

the selfless bliss of the body

i

somewhere, under skirts
of black, a nun brings
herself to orgasm,
making love with the christ-
nature of her hand, her husband.
as toes tighten, white thighs
tremble, she closes her eyes
and dies and dies with him
in the selfless bliss
of the body

ii

speaking your name,
i feel myself spiral
into my body as my voice
spirals out, uncovering,
discovering, the space
between my bones, swollen
with my small history,
empty, happy

iii

the body is a verb, not a noun:
even in a monk's stillness,
the circle of breath, twist
of double helix, turns
always turns
towards its absence,
towards the empty body
of pure vibration

My Aunt's Shoulders

Rochelle goes to the beauty
salon every week,
the lather and comb
a well anticipated caress,
the only other hands
her body knows.

I offer a neck rub. Rochelle
accepts. Her shoulders
are a child's, hard, untouched.
I am overcome with a sweet ache
to release them; I want to give and give
from my fingers, my palms, my wrists,
until her shoulders open
and allow themselves to be
shoulders, not thoughts of shoulders,
but real live shoulders,
the lovable nerve and the bone.

X-Tasy

(Two abecedarians)

1.

Apple brownbetty cures depression.
Eat fruit generously; hunger is just
kindling, lurking minutes north
of pleasure. Quit rationing;
start tasting unlimited varieties,
wanting x-tasy, yumminess, zest.

2.

All bodies create desire.
    Enlivened flesh gives
        hot, insistent juice.
            Kissed lips may not obey
                propriety; quiet rustlings
                    spawn tempestuous undulations—
                      vroom!
                          —wild x-tasy, yowling zeniths

Scratch Test

The inner forearm
is a tender place. When you slide
your fingertips from my wrist
to the crook of my elbow,
the backs of my knees tighten
and twist like the insides
of camera lenses. Picture

the allergist's needle, scratching
fine lines into that thin forearm skin,
dripping in potential poison—
mold, dust, pollen, fur. All
of it rose in angry mosquito
bite bubbles—I was allergic
to everything, even grass,
even trees. The doctor measured
the weal and flare of each blister,
dutifully recorded every centimeter
of response on a stiff white card. I
wanted to peel the itchy skin
from my arm, wave its bumpy
stretch like a flag—I surrender,
no more. He understood, gave
me a tissue soaked with alcohol
to sting the itch away.

I want to know what makes you
itch. I want to hold your arm down
on my lap, take a needle, scratch
my initials into your skin. I want
to drip my saliva, your sweat,
everything unspoken between
us—into the slit and see
what rises up. I want
you to surrender. I want
to measure the weal and flare.

Bread and Butter

for Michael

I often wonder how people figured
things out—simple things like bread
and butter. How did the first person know
to grind and knead and bake,
to milk and skim and churn?
How did someone realize they could soak
olives in lye or let grape juice ferment
inside casks of oak? How, when
we first leaned toward each other,
did our tongues know to touch
before our brains knew
we were going to kiss at all?

shot through

the sprinkler, the oil
puddle, shot through
with rainbow
like muddle-mind shot
with pure thought;
the precise angle,
a clear angel—spectral,
joy-like—touch
shooting through nerve
at the right angle
so the body
is shot through
with light

FLORA

Mano in Fica

After many naked weeks,
our fig tree is growing hands;
five-fingered leaves
sprout from the tip
of each thin limb,
knuckles pliant,
curved to cup the sun.

Too small
to cover
nakedness,
these leaves would nestle
in Eve's pubic hair
like emeralds,
clasp her nipples
with their bright palms,
vegetable fingers
brushing gates
of paradise.

*

In Italy, if you thrust
a thumb through the cleft
between two fingers,
you make *fig hand,*
mano in fica,
potent as flipping the bird.
Fica you, it says, *fica off,*
Adam and Eve banished
from the garden.
In India, the same gesture
is a sacred mudra,
yoni and lingam joined
in perfect union,

lost in the Eden of flesh.

*

In our backyard,
the fig leaves
open their fists.
They grasp nothing
but the air around
their new green skin,
dream of nothing
but sugar and gravity,
wave hello
to the same breeze
that will strip
their wrists bare.

Choking

The neighbors' artichokes peek
over the fence, spiny verdigris heads
thatched with lilac hair.
They smolder like grenades,
send vague threats
across the redwood slats.
I thought artichokes
grew like melons—armadillos
snuffling against the earth—
but these punk buds
are air born, wavering
high and top heavy
on their tendony stalks,
daring me to lob off their heads,
dance them onto a plate,
tear off their stiff veils
one by dusky one until I find
the damp vegetable fur,
the fibrous button,
the bitter and buttery heart.

Jacaranda

You can hear the blossoms
or maybe taste them
before they enter your sight—
the purple vibrates at some
frequency the body
can barely understand.
Only your peripheral vision
can process the color
that glows from the trees—
ultra violet, maybe,
a fine tuned hum,
a shade so tender
it hurts the eyes.

*

Jacaranda flowers smell
like honey and piss;
It's hard to tell
if the heavy scent
that cloaks the public
library comes
from the abundance
of purple blossoms
in the parking lot,
or from the people
who relieve themselves
against the side
of the building.

*

Each pod
on the jacaranda tree
looks like a beak

from some mean
and leathery bird.
but from these coarse,
sharp-tipped
mouths float
the most delicate
words.

Flora

I've always liked the term
"lily-livered." I know it means
cowardly, but this is how
I see it: the liver, sleek
and wine-colored, bursts forth
with lilies; petals drift
and ride the streams of blood.
Think of it: the body
opens into flower, turns orchid-
spleened, jasmine-lunged, breath
tropical, humid with scent.
Poppies bloom between the legs,
wisteria vines wind
up the spine, each bone filled
with pollen and sweet nectar. The heart
is a rose, of course, plushly
blossomed, and inside the skull,
with each new thought,
a tulip unfurls
in the brain.

Pear

The pear is like a stone at first,
a monk sitting zazen
on my desk. I could never break through
its skin of concentration—
even its scent eludes me,
though I admire the still,
silent focus of its body.
Soon the pear begins to soften,
becomes a woman, a goddess
by my computer, hips swelling
voluptuous and proud. Her fragrance
wafts towards me as she ripens,
wrapping the sweetness of her body
around the air around my head,
pulling herself into my nostrils,
my senses full of her emanations.
The goddess ages, becomes her true self
before my eyes, a fruit
that darkens, ferments,
works its way back to the earth,
a slow melt that echoes
my own body's passage,
the deliciousness of its undoing.

Onions

for Catherine

Last Sunday, thousands of people
looted three onion warehouses
in Northern India,
grabbing pungent globes
by the armful, trailing
papery bronze skins
behind them
like scraps of their own hands.
Onions, potatoes, salt,
have been in short supply there,
have been hoarded by sellers
who jack up the prices,
turning staples scarce and precious,
turning people into wild, hungry, tongues,
rioting for their human right
to taste.

*

Yesterday, tv news coverage
of Hurricane Mitch
showed a man stumbling
up a steep, eroded, slope,
tightly gripping a block of onions
tied together like a bale of hay.
The slender amethyst bulbs gleamed
like Christmas tree ornaments
among their long green sprouts.
The man had carried the onions
for over forty miles
so the survivors of his village
could have something, anything,
to eat. The crunch, the burn,

of those onions must have brought
them back into themselves a bit,
must have reminded them
that they were still alive,
although their eyes looked too stunned
to be stung by the sharp fumes
released between their teeth.

*

"I am whirling this week," you write,
"I am an onion this week. We all
seem to go through layers of self-
knowing." I soak your words in
the way an onion soaks up oil,
turning translucent and tender
over the flame.
How lucky I am
to have you as a friend.
How lucky we are,
how goddamned privileged,
to be able to go buy onions
so easily. There must be
fifteen stores within five miles
of our safe homes
where we can buy them—brown, white, red,
Sweet Vidalia, Hawaiian, pearl,
for just a few dimes a pound.
How lucky, how almost embarrassingly
fortunate we are
to have the basic outer resources
that give us the luxury
to look inward,
peeling away at our layers
like so many glittering scarves
while only a few countries away,

people are packed under mud
like root vegetables,
while across the ocean,
people are crazed
for simple sustenance—
onions, potatoes, salt.

*

The first poem I wrote in college
was about onions, about peeling onions.
All I remember of it is this line,
repeated throughout the poem:
"Where is the core?"
In the poem, I kept peeling and peeling,
never finding what lay at the center,
although in my mind I pictured
a small pearly bud there,
like an iridescent jewel,
or a sexual nub,
or a heart.
A few months later, I peeled
a real onion,
and I found that there *was* no core,
that the whole thing
was built around
a small chamber of air.
It is this place
I fall into
when I hear about suffering
in India, in Nicaragua,
my own town, anywhere,
this pit that aches
like raw onion heartburn.
I try to claw myself out

by sending what I can
to relief funds,
by sending out my prayers,
but I still feel surrounded
by stinking white walls.
Your words help guide me
through the slippery layers
back to the world
where the real work
has yet to be done.

SWARM

jellyfish

it was a big year for jellyfish,
la niña pulling them
like magnets to the shore.
a fresh translucent mass
was heaped every few feet
along the beach—
edges scalloped
like flamenco skirts,
some hemmed
with thready purple—
the poison ones,
we learned from chris,
who used to have jellyfish fights
with her friends in massachusetts.
didn't they sting you? i asked,
remembering horror stories
of foot stings, leg stings,
vinegar poultices,
but she said no, they knew
which were safe to lob
at each other,
the creatures smacking
against their bodies
in brief wet flashes
like living artificial breasts.

the beached jellyfish
did look like saline implants—
a vast exodus of implants
on the lam from tinseltown,
panting their freedom
into the great bosom of sand.
i could almost hear chests deflate
up and down the sunset strip,
could almost hear

a chorus of nipples
sigh in soft relief
as one buoyant sack
after another slid
out of its mammary cave
and flopped its way back
to the sea.

later i saw jellyfish
swimming in the harbor,
their flounces
billowing in and out
like valves of a blowsy heart.
jellyfish have no heart, no gills,
no brain—they are all undulation,
all open mouth. i wanted to scoop
them out of the water,
plaster them over my breasts,
let them harpoon my areolas
with their stinging cells
the way my nursing children
would clamp their jaws
around my nipples
when they first began to teethe—
la niña, el niño, returned to me
as babies, their suckling skulls
all fontanel, bells of milky light.

Desired by Ants

The ants want me. For the second
time this week, they swarm the panties
crumpled on the floor as I
shower. They congregate in
the crotch, hundreds of tiny bodies;
they lap up my drippings
like honey. If I slipped
that underwear on, how would it feel,
literal ants in the pants?
Would they climb up inside me,
plumb the candy apple
of my cervix, would they curl
deep in my pubic hair? The thought
does not turn me on. But insects
desire me. When I go outside,
it is my arms the mosquitoes drill,
my ankles the fleas attack, every
one else unscathed. "It's because
you're so sweet," my mom used to say,
but I don't know...Sometimes I think
flies buzz around me because
they think I'm dead.

I would love to have butterflies
flap halos around my head, dragonflies
tickle at my elbows, fire flies
turn my palms to lanterns,
but it is the base bug
that wants me, the insect
you try to step on, swat, shoo
away, it is the monster bug
that smells wild sugar
in my skin.

Swarm

The bees hang
from the branch
in a buzzing clump,
a dark organ near
the entrance of the pool
at our mother's new complex,
my sister's and my first visit
here. No hive surrounds them,
no honeycomb—just a droning lobe
draped from the tree.

We gape at the feral
bulb, bigger than
our heads. Lone bees
fly in, wiggle towards
the center, add to the din.
We are scared to get too close,
scared our kids will get stung,
but we can't tear ourselves away—
how often do we see
wildness like this
in such careful landscaping?
It's as if everything we want
to say to our mom
has burst from our bodies,
all those hidden, roiling words
finding form before our eyes.

Later at the pool,
we feel splashes
on our cheeks and arms.
Not water; these drops
are warm and orange, thick
as paint all over our skin.
A pixilated cloud hovers

above the pool, bees
risen from the tree, dropping
pollen juice, nectar bombs,
rasping the air electric.
Our kids fly screaming
from the water; we wrap
them in towels and sprint
to our mother's clean apartment,
dripping florid, indelible orange.

Caddis

upon seeing photos of Hubert Duprat's jewel-encrusted Caddisfly larvae

The artist lays pearls before larvae,
lays pearls and turquoise and flakes
of gold before caddisfly
larvae who, in the wild, wrap
themselves with fishbone
and driftwood and sand
bound with silk from their bodies,
build protective sleeping
bags of grit. The artist watches
larvae gather jewels,
build glittering sarcophagi
around their humble brown
bodies, bands of opal set
between intricate shingles
of gold. When the larvae grow
wings and leave these jeweled
tubes behind, the artist will slip
them over his fingers like thimbles, like olives,
his own tiny pharaonic shrouds.

Geodes
-or-
An ode to VCCA

On the cow-flanked road
between bed and desk, a patch
of asphalt has fallen away,
exposing large chunks of quartz
beneath, as if the road itself
is a geode, broken into
radiance. We all break open
here—"I had a breakthrough today,"
I hear again and again, from writer,
from artist, from composer, each of us
cracking through the stone skin
of our lives to find hidden minerals
that startle with their color, their ability
to catch the light. One day, I opened
my studio door to find the room full
of ladybugs, walls seething with them,
air alive with specks of red, and I knew
my own heart had burst open there,
coating every surface with its jagged,
winged, hum.

Beard of Bees

They tickle until they don't,
all those tiny legs, all
that whirring. It's like having
your face inside a wind
tunnel, but gentle, like being
a tv screen rimmed with warm
static. It makes you feel
you can fly, your head lifting
from your body like a balloon
released from its string.
And when they sting,
as they do, it hurts
no more than love.

WAITING

Side Stepping

Don't step on a crack
or you'll break
your mama's back;
don't step on a line
or you'll break
your mama's spine;
don't step on a red tile
in the lobby of your father's
office building
or you'll die a fiery
death; don't step
on a white tile
in the bathroom
of the train station
or you'll surely freeze;
don't step past the photo
of the girl who died
that's hanging near
your cousin's bedroom
or you'll wind up
sick like her; don't step
off the curb when you're waiting
for your parents to pick you up
or the station wagon will crash
en route; don't step
on the earth itself
or one day you'll turn
to dust.

Telemetry

The nurse squeezes clear goo
onto three round patches,
then attaches them to my skin—
two near my clavicle, one on my belly—
making me a many-nippled
Athena. My heartbeat
travels through these numb
areolae, through the wires
that spring from their perky points,
to a monitor two floors below.
I wonder what it looks like,
my heartbeat, the scritch
of its rhythm, to the stranger
who reads it somewhere under my bed,
my life distilled to one thin line—
a rise and fall, a simple scrawl—
much like this ink I drag
across the page.

On Waiting for My Husband's X-Ray Results

Here's to bones,
the way they build
themselves inside
our mothers' wombs,
the way they hold us
together, keep us
in line. Here's to those
hollow flutes, those
marrow tubes, the
closest we get
to branch and stone.
Here's to our architecture,
our scaffolding, the bare
beams of our bodies
that will remain long after
our bodies melt away,
Here's to the ribs
that hold our tender
hearts, the pelvis
that cradles our love.
Here's to the wrist
that brings your hand
to my face, the wrist
that makes you
cringe, the wrist
that will knit itself
back together
just as surely as it
did when it first
named itself wrist,
that graceful swivel
of bone.

On Waiting to Find Out if a Mole on My Son's Back is Malignant

If a pregnant woman craves a food
but doesn't eat it, according to Italian lore,
the child will be born with a birthmark
in the shape of that food. One woman's
son was born with a triangular blotch
on his forehead—proof, she swears,
she should have eaten that slice of pizza
she had hungered for. She calls the mole
a *voglia*—a longing, a craving left to fester,
her child marked by her unmet desire
for yeast, tomato, oily ribbons of cheese.

What did I crave, what did I deny myself,
that sent this spray across my son's
chest and back, his neck,
as if truck tires had spattered
him with clots of puddle mud?
Had my vegetarian blood lusted
for burgers, meatballs, malt balls—
food dark and thick and round
as my pale belly swelled
with borrowed light? Or do these marks
tell of another gnawing, the worry
I forced to the pit of my stomach,
wondering whether I was ready
to be a young mother, a good mother;
did these fears fester unspoken
in my throat, did they travel
deeper, etching themselves into his sweet
forming skin? How could I have known
how ready I would be?
How could I have known
I could never be ready
for what this map might mean,
this smattering of angel kisses,
this constellation of dark stars?

Super Powers

My daughter can speak with the wind.
She learned how to do this
at the beach; *The water and the wind
are friends*, she says. *You have
to make friends with them
if you want to be safe.*

I want her to be safe.
I've been having bad dreams
about her almost every night
lately—bullet to the head,
chemotherapy, accidents
in the street, coffins on the ready—
and I'm trying to tell myself
it's not a sign, not an omen
that something horrible
is about to happen

I am learning my super powers,
she says. *A book hit me in the eye,
and ever since then, I can see with my
eyes closed. I've been waiting to figure out
my super powers for a long time.*

I've been waiting to write this poem
a long time. I worry—if I write
my fears down, will I make them
happen? Am I writing an epitaph?
Is that my super power?
Or if I write these dreams,
(and this is what I hope)
will I break their spell,
strip their power away?

The elements used to be people,

she says. *Only the chosen people*
Turn into elements when they die.
She is one of the chosen people,
she tells me, so certain of her power.

Let me never find out if this is true.
Let me never have to listen
to the wind and wonder
if my daughter is
whispering
in my ear.

Waiting Outside Radiology

It's good practice for being dead.
They wheel you on a gurney
from your hospital room down
to radiology, park you in an alcove
beside two other gurneys
where people in matching gowns
also wait to be scanned. The orderlies
talk over your silent heads about a girl
they both dated. You are just bodies
to them, not interesting bodies
like the girl in question, just bodies
to be wheeled from one place
to another. Your faces might as well be
covered with sheets. It's not so bad,
really. It's good to remember life
will go on without you. Still, when
they finally bring you into the x-ray room
and give you the choice between lying
down or sitting for the 15 minute
intervals between films, you sit up
because you still can.

WORLDLING

worldling

*(1549): a person engrossed in the
concerns of this present world*

What other world
should we be
engrossed in?
What other world
should concern us?
Even when we turn
to the past, press
toward the future,
our bodies are in this
present world, here
in this present
world, all of us
worldlings, hatchlings
testing squawk
and feet and feathers
as the earth
keeps us close
to her breast.

Climbing at Joshua Tree

The rock will hold your hand,
but you have to work for it,
fingers hunting for that gritty
ridge, that sharp ledge that will
accept your weight, help you
pull your sticky soled shoes
up to the next subtle foothold.
The world disappears as you
climb, becomes nothing more
than the sun on your back, the rock
before you, its face impassive,
unimpressed, as your muscles
seize and burn. But that's what
the desert is, isn't it? Life boiled
down to its most basic parts:
sun and stone and the twitch
of survival. And when you hoist
yourself up to the top of the rock,
each limb trembling, throat
a dry ache, the desert offers up
its lunar landscape, its shaggy
prehistoric trees, a sky so big
it jars your skull, so big you have
to lie flat and let the heat
of the rock seep through
your shirt, let its steady presence
ground you before you
make the trip back down.

Buttered Women

The Nicaraguan poet speaks
of battered women, but her vowels
are round and wet, and I hear (I want
to hear) *buttered. Buttered women,*
like potatoes, green beans,
toast, women buttered
to a fevered, golden, sheen.
So many women—one every nine
seconds—slathered with sweet
and salted yellow cream,
pats smeared over their ribs, knees,
shoulder blades, bits melting
into each warm fold, bits blinking
like sequins from their hair.
So much easier to picture women
dripping with comfort; so much
easier to imagine a world
where no hand is lifted except
to butter a piece of bread, a breast.
I imagine the buttered women's
shelter (what I think I hear her
say, what I wish I hear her say)
must smell like breakfast,
sunny eggs and pancakes,
all those hot buttered women
gleaming in their skins.

Coast Starlight

Hello! the old man yells
from the seat in front of us.
Hello! to the window every five minutes or so,
jostling us from books, from talk, from sleep.

Hello! LA River graffiti.
Hello! Pastures of cows.
Hello! Llamas and lumber mills and clotheslines.

Hello! When a car flips onto the tracks.
Hello! When the train starts up again two hours later.

40 hours of *Hello!* up the entire West Coast,
through farmland and forest,
darkness and mountain, and we don't change
our seats when given the chance
because how often do we get to hear someone
greet each inch of the world?

His *Hello!* punctuated only b*y Jesus
Christ!* and *Where am I?*
and, when we pass the ocean,
IT'S SO BEAUTIFUL!

Billow and Flume

I often wonder what happened
to my mother's molecules
after we dumped her ashes
into the Oceanside Harbor
and watched them billow
and flume like jellyfish
or atomic explosions
under water, a gorgeous
expansion of gray. Are
the molecules that were once
her eyes splitting the distance
between Hawaii and Japan?
Are bits of her clavicle in Baja,
atoms of her heart traveling
through the belly of a whale
near Antarctica, parts of her
big toe washing up on
the Australian shore? Did
shards of one hip bone tango
down to South America,
portions of the other shimmy
up to the Bering Strait?
Does a molecule from her
liver ever swim past a molecule
from her throat and think
yes, yes, I once knew you?

Last Words

A movie villain claimed
people say one of two things
when they're about to die—
Jesus or *Shit*. I doubt this
will be me. When I'm
in trouble, confused, having
a hard time, a voice bubbles
in my skull, says *I love you*.
I don't know who is speaking—
a god I'm not sure exists?
My mom? Some channel
of self-comfort?—but the voice
is clear and bright as a star,
a spark, saying words
I hope will pass through my lips
when it's my time, my love
for the world riding
my last breath—*I love you*
I love you I love you

Gayle Brandeis is the author of *Fruitflesh: Seeds of Inspiration for Women Who Write* (HarperOne) and the novels *The Book of Dead Birds* (HarperCollins), which won the Bellwether Prize for Fiction of Social Engagement (judged by Toni Morrison, Maxine Hong Kingston, and contest founder Barbara Kingsolver), Self Storage (Ballantine), Delta Girls (Ballantine), and My Life with the Lincolns (Henry Holt), which received a Silver Nautilus Book Award and was chosen as a state wide read in Wisconsin. Her memoir, *The Art of Misdiagnosis*, is forthcoming from Beacon Press. Her essays, poems and short fiction have been widely published in places such as *Salon, The Rumpus, The Nervous Breakdown* and *The Mississippi Review,* and have received numerous honors, including a Barbara Mandigo Kelly Peace Poetry Award, the *QPB/Story Magazine* Short Story Award, and a Notable mention in *The Best American Essays* 2016. She teaches in the BA and low residency MFA programs at Sierra Nevada College, where she was named Distinguished Visiting Professor/Writer in Residence, and the low residency MFA program at Antioch University, Los Angeles. Gayle served as Inlandia Literary Laureate from 2012-2014 and was called a Writer Who Makes a Difference by *The Writer Magazine.* She lives in North Lake Tahoe.

CPSIA information can be obtained
at www.ICGtesting.com
Printed in the USA
BVOW11s0726161117
500168BV00002B/340/P